NOT TO

New & Selected Poems

NOT TO

New & Selected Poems

Elaine Terranova

THE SHEEP MEADOW PRESS
RIVERDALE-ON-HUDSON, NEW YORK

All inquiries and permission requests should be addressed to:
The Sheep Meadow Press
P.O. Box 1345
Riverdale-on-Hudson, NY 10471

Designed and typeset by The Sheep Meadow Press.
Distributed by The University Press of New England.

Printed on acid-free paper in the United States. This book meets the guidelines for permanence and durability of the Committee on Production Guidelines for Book Longevity of the Council on Library Resources.

Library of Congress Cataloging-in-Publication Data

Terranova, Elaine
  Not to : poems / by Elaine Terranova.
     p. cm.
  ISBN 1-931357-32-3 (alk. paper)
  I. Title.

PS3570.E6774N67 2006
811'.54--dc22

2006006320

To L.H.C.

CONTENTS

Not To (new poems)

from The Dog's Heart (2002)

from Damages (1996)

from The Cult of the Right Hand (1991)

from Toward Morning/Swimmers (1980)

NOT TO (new poems)

NOT TWO   I

PREVIEW

I mention the dead woman
on the bench in Rittenhouse Square
all those years ago. You say
you saw her too. I had to ask
a bystander, I couldn't quite
take it in. The police had cordoned off
a wedge of park, a statue and a pool
she could have been looking at.
Do you ever think of those still-open eyes?
Leaves were thick on the ground.
I remember the disturbance they made.
You passed and I passed. It was a time
we might have met. But more
important to me now is that, before
we once laid eyes on each other,
we should have stood together
staring down at this.

EIDOLON

Helen never went to Troy,
Zeus dispatched a double of her there
to foment strife and bloodshed among men.
—Euripides' *Electra*

I never saw the cows' breath curl
as they grazed the cold mountain.
They never lifted their eyes to me
over the wooden slope of their shoulders.
Nothing borrowed me from sleep.
Time didn't register, the events
that strike anywhere minute by minute.
An idol in the clouds held my place.
I felt nothing, not even pain,
which may be a way the world
comes to you, if not the right way.
The Scamander in flame? The war god
come off the Greek ships in search of me?

What I dreamt was motion only,
butterflies or wind. I woke
to the shuttling ocean. More green
it was than blue. Sandpipers drilled,
turning toward shore, and I followed
the arrows of their footprints.
This was Egypt and off in a corner,
lay fierce Asia. He never took me,
that king's son, that player of the lyre.
The goddess' promise had no substance.
His arms closed over air.

LE MÉPRIS

In movies, life is only
a particular set of circumstances.
So, in *Contempt* (*Le Mépris*), that film
of Godard's, a screenwriter's wife
stops loving him. They have spent
the morning in bed, she asking,
"Do you like my ass?" "Do you like
my breasts?" "Yes," he answers,
"Yes," as if trying to determine
what the real question is. She is,
of course, trying to pin him down,
to place a value on herself, lot
by lot, like real estate. This is
cinemascope, and Brigitte Bardot
plays the wife. The man finds himself
surrounded by her as if she were
all of creation. But when
he sends her off with the producer
in the man's red Alpha,
all she feels for her husband
is contempt. The couple can't go on
past this, beyond wandering through
unpaneled doors of their new apart-
ment. The Mediterranean
stretches out its smooth blue body
alongside Bardot. They are making a film
of *The Odyssey*—we have to think
of Penelope—and there are zooms
to stone gods, their eyes painted shut.
With just 149 shots,
Godard, half-God, concentrates
on the important things,

love and death, as the screenwriter
might himself. He kills off the wife
and her new friend in that sports car.
No need to, really. She'd never
have left, holding on as if everything
were still in place, contempt
from time to time whipping back
in their faces like a sharp gust.

MINT

Already, we'd be driving past
those trees, that part of the forest.
Even briefly, it refreshed you.
It was like mint in August
though that sting would be gone
with summer. The ground
tarnishing first, and soon the leaves.
I thought then, men don't stop.
They want so much to get on.
What we said, incidental
yet hammered into the mind.
Talk like a magnet, so it draws you
together or away. We made a line
around that part of the forest,
the exact shape of our attention.
Even after, I remember
how it was taken up and moved
along with us, into the dim
living room. Each holding a glass,
ice colliding in water. A tiny
mirrored sun caught in the trees.
The same sadness that darkened
our features. Later, bed
without making love, without
the chance of a reprieve.

SHEEP

Look down from your height
to the pasture, while the sheep
bend to the grass,
thickening wool and flesh for winter.
Bodies so abrupt at the end, without tails,
like limbs they have lost.

You may want
to undress. You may want to urinate,
send yourself in that stream down to them.

White mornings he and I
went out in the car
far into the country to look for them.
They clustered beside us,
fences were nothing, one by one
letting us pat their heads, wanting
to be counted or blessed.

And why should they know how it is
in the world, soon the man in a suit,
the jacketed carcass. The woman
bereft, nakedly weeping.

DECEIT

The word reminding me
of a murder mystery.
Or of hunting—
decoys, traps, blinds. Something,
someone, being stalked. A door
snapped shut on a red hush.
I mention a man I loved,
what he tried to keep from me.
I'd seen an envelope
he said was "a business matter,"
though the return address
might have been written
by a fourteen-year-old girl,
circle-dotted i's, no name on top.
And his disappearances. I'd call
hour after hour, imagine him
slumped under the phone,
receiver in his hand, a heart attack.
All night, busy signals.
The telephone company
assured me nothing was wrong,
but night is a time of warning
and I knew, I knew. My body felt empty,
nothing going on in it
but a dry flutter, a flushed bird.

BREAK

The rain would stop, then begin again.
In this the day was adamant.
And in between, fog,
where so much dropped out,
unnecessary.

She lowered the volume
so that the radio sounded
like a little toy radio

and thought of the break
of waves, the break in a bone,
simple or compound,
like a reckless sentence.

Thought, this is how the world
is presented, swiftly, as if
from a train. At night, had almost
replaced sleep with reading,

wondering why the body means
so much, what it marks. So they
would separate, like dice cast,

not a couple, not toted up
together anymore, but left
wherever they settled.

The letter, deep in his desk
or the pocket of a jacket.
He hadn't the wish or the foresight
to wad it up, milling it

between fingertips to the girth of a pea,
and even so, she'd have felt it,
insistent, under the mattress
where they lay.

THE ANNIVERSARY

That night
  the comet could still be seen,
  wound in its wild mane.

Earlier, an egret
  had stopped by the stream
  to clean itself of something,
  red bill dipping
  again and again
  into the white feathers.

And before that,
  walking along,
  we became aware
  of a tiny, fragile skeleton
  at the side of the road,
  paws drawn up
  over its empty chest.

REMEMBER

how at its edges water is always sighing.
Think of the lake as it curves, cloud eye
at its center. The polished surface
laying a clear varnish
over the future.

        Then sunset,
the night's first misfortune. Those
fuchsia orchids rushing out of the vase,
anything burning, in exile. People who live
in furnished houses, who move from chair
to chair to find the best light.

Sometime, you would have to let the fresh air in,
knowing something else has gone on here.
And what noise you'd make, music
on the radio, the looping saxophone.
Someone upstairs, maybe imagined, who gets
disgusted, shuts a book. And below,

lovers who turn to one another as if
there is no one else, until sleep becomes
the one thing holding them together.

SUNDOWNER

The day is sinking, maybe forever.
Now there is only the monotone
of night. Nothing belongs to me.
Not a house, not a person.

Flowers paper the walls
with stillness. If I listen
I hear a hundred legger
whisper against the floorboards.
Then that screamer begins next door.
A sound like ball bearings
reverberates in her throat.

The human voice, as if
it were important. I think how bad
I am at telling stories, everyone's eyes
on my mouth. Talk is a monument.
Things walk in the halls
of a word. I'm not sure, though,

that there is anything to say. Maybe
you and I find words for whatever passes,
birds and animals at the window,
crying out for names. Leaves

that wave in the breeze to get
our attention. We have to think
of something as we go, holding onto
the two handles of our burden.

LATE AFTERNOON

Oh see the gorgeous, warring clouds.
I am expecting distant music,
familiar, though. The circus
or a concert in a park. Someone passes
who almost knows me. How the winter
disguises us, she says. And it's true,
the body can be mistaken,
no matter how purely it cries out.
Yet it is scarcely winter,
crocuses up already
in the lawns where no one cares.

Think how it was before I left.
We couldn't take each other anywhere,
we were so terribly out of step.
Later, there would be a broken moon,
and from the train, clusters of tiny lights
like a rash, the towns left behind.
I imagined night's loud footsteps,
our house waking without me,
that yawn in the bed, one side gone

and other things I can't name, I can't
be held responsible for.

KNOT TWO   II

THE QUESTION

That winter night, the East Village
in the '50s. Moment shaved from the solid wood
of a life. Outside, the dark accumulated.
I was waiting for the moon to rise and focus
everything. A Japanese restaurant. Steam on the windows
like our own warmth condensing. What we were,
young and friends and didn't know how to be lovers.
That bare room like the bare room of my heart.

Meanwhile, the only other people, a couple
back from the window, kneeled on the clean tatami,
leaning together. They showed us what desire is.
Think of her long red hair. Their knees touched,
they were a single piece carved from the same stuff.
Too far to hear I saw the half-smile, an answer
to something being asked. A rice paper screen
shielded them, its plum branch left of center
dipped and rose like a checkmark.

It comes back to me, the way the wish
surrounds you. It's your body
and you can't leave it alone, you keep
pouring feeling into it. Only when you look up
from your life like that are you aware
of anyone else. Of how to ask for love,
to ask for permission.

HUNTER'S MOON

Darkness was always toppling me
into someone's bed. A year of lost umbrellas.
How could I keep track of where
it had rained? Anyhow, it was the moon
I remembered. It splashed over fields,

immortalizing the screech owl
and the shrew, the pearl jaws of whatever
lay in the road. How later it became
sort of ellipsoid, flat, you know, the way
the moon gets. Deflated, hung over a branch.

Eerie, that lane of hibiscus,
moonfaced, pale, with their choked,
dark centers. I think then I believed in ghosts,
in someone who left behind only fingerprints,
furniture that wouldn't budge.

Every part of my body woke
to its own identifying pleasure or pain.
All new. Like cut wood
with that liberated smell, hay or manure,
something not yet in the world.

WHAT WEIGHS

Damsel-
or dragonflies,
nearly transparent.
Hook and eye, they hold on.

An extension ladder,
continuing one another. She,
caught at head or thorax, climbing
the devil's long waistcoat.

Yes, like that, to be towed,
an inscription in air.
Adhering.

Kisses like nails.
An arm bracing my shoulder,
my head flung back
as if I were leaning
over a balcony.
But nothing weighs
like the gummy flesh.

While she is seized, tipped
toward his sperm.
Surprise, as the basis
of the tango is surprise.

Afterward,
she sheds eggs into water.
The nymphs rise,
lower lip folded back
over the tiny mad face
like an outlaw's mask.

INVITATION

You said, "I like your husband.
How long have you been together?"
Which was an invitation to say more, the way
we got together, why. But my answer
was like a stone skipping water, the speed,
the eerie sound it made: "Four years."
What I should have said is that we met
the summer I turned forty. That there
had been three men, that one was marrying
someone else. I thought I'd put him
at the side of my life, on a back burner,
I told my friend, though I kept
the taste of his name in my mouth.
Another, younger than I, had written
Happy Birthday on a card forty times,
then called one night, suicidal. "I can't
be alone," he said. A poor connection. I swore
I heard the stammer of the rain. But it
was only his voice knocking on the wooden dark.
I hadn't gone. So there was just my husband,
after all, left real. And what I remember most
about that summer was a time he wasn't there,
before I'd even begun thinking of him
when he wasn't there. A picnic at the Lakes
by a narrow, gingerbread bridge
built for an exposition and other structures
now abandoned, nearly falling down.
My friend's friend, the magician, sat beside me,
making an egg appear and disappear. Something
was bothering him, something was wrong. His girl,
an Amazonian blonde from the Midwest,
she was an actress, kept going to the water's edge

and looking in. His trick was like a secret
future of company, a way of drawing
someone to you. It was like the sun
skittering behind clouds as it had that day,
making our surroundings seem to appear
and disappear, the dull grass and white bedspread
over it. This must have been a Sunday.
I was thinking of a job I wanted
and whether they, or anyone,
would call the next morning.

IN A COUPLE

When you were young love
so often muted you. Though now
you see the point of conversation
may be to give each other courage.

You pass along a book you've read,
something with closure, so that
he too can be relieved for a little
of his restlessness. Or point out

how the snow that was promised
has somehow been forfeited. Say
anything. For the children of friends

have come to look like their impostors.
And where is the sun that rushed out
to greet you? Now for cheer, only
the careless rubbings of the moon.

Meanwhile, your words are
tolling you in and out of each other's
concentration. Listen. What it means,
I love you and Why, requiring

incessant repetition. As when
you are very young, an infant,
there's that moment of recognition:
the eyes open, the translation begins.

EASTERN DAYLIGHT TIME

In the distance, a cross-hatch of trees.
Sparrows weave in and out.
So small. They seem to move so quickly.

It's spring, the first green, just tacked
to the ground and those young men, her children,
home again. She'd loved so much the soft,
unfinished faces, perfect now, nearly shining.

The sun is stiffening her skin, the breeze
buffets her where she stands,
can't let her alone. Each day brings
its own peculiarities.
There is no hope of the banal.
This cascade of cherry blossoms, for instance,
branches taking deep breaths, rising and falling,

and these young men who might be gods or strangers.
They have so little to say,
with their own children now, babies they must watch
every minute. A table is set up on the lawn.
She lays along it silver that catches the sun,
a feast that rolls on and on. Only moments before

she and her husband passed on to a grandchild
all the songs they remembered. She hated
her voice, her Philadelphia accent.

And suddenly she thinks, Why, we're lightening,
passing from sight. So that what they'd sung
seems the om of creation, destruction, release.
Which is all right. All right,
if it would end that way, and they could begin again.

COMMUNE

We watched, at night, stars drop
into the pocket of the lake. By day

wandered off to the blueberry patch.
I loved that we could lose each other,
the way the thicket

pulled you aside,
subtracted you from the world.
A darkness you could see through,
shading like a bruise.

Smooth shoots, close
and twining. Staggering
at their different heights. Wild,
the way animals are wild. We'd go,
sons or stepsons, daughters, wives.

The first fruit startled the empty pail
or pan, tin measuring cup.
Spilling over,
you can only contain so much. As joy
is a filling up and an overflow.

Blue stuck to us, everyone
had that tattoo,
the same genealogy at the tip

of the tongue.
On its own, the blueberry
is reclusive as a nun.
Two separate species needed
for them to propagate.

When they do, as now,
they have no restraint, bearing
all that they can,
offering themselves up to you.

STARWATCH

Here we are far enough
from the bright impatient city,
so our friend sets up
his telescope in a field.
Alone, I couldn't undo the knots of light
like this, even if I tried to keep
enough darkness in my head

but he is guiding us.
We look, as we are told,
for "close pairs," like us,
bound by force or chance. Dead stars above us,
stars not yet born, the rest of that

boiling light. I shiver
as he reaches across my shoulder,
adjusting the sights.
And for a minute, each star
is stilled in its glass cage,
though above, it goes on beating.

"The seeing," he says, "is good tonight."
He points out Orion, the hunter,
and the Pleiades, sister doves,
wings flapping silver and black,
who have come to rest
in Orion's belt.

Like any speech,
what leaves his mouth
is absolute freedom, absolute determinism,
his breath reminding me how

my husband's pursed lips
strike my neck
with the fricatives of sleep.

Each star is cold and stinging,
an animal eye that looks back into your eye,
the only speech it has.
I am staring up at tears in the sky,
minor imperfections,
starlight trickling down to us,
that trigger to the heart.

NOT TO **III**

"THE HEAP"

When I come in they're reading
right to left, back to front,
undoing all they ever learned.
I do it too, reciting
as if fish bones are stuck in my throat.

Soon we are giggling. Sweat breaks out
above our Hebrew teacher's lips.
I know he would like to pinch our arms
but is careful not to. Little girls,
we might be another species.

I stare at that width of starched white shirt
across his belly, bow tie
tying off what's animal. I imagine
a patch of skin I must once have seen,
puckered and hairy, like elephant skin.

In Hebrew one word is over all.
You crave it and are not allowed
even to make the sound of it.
A word that brings life out of dust.

In my comic book, a dead GI in camouflage
comes back a walking compost heap.
If you're reborn, it must be because
the world has not had enough of you.

So many odd things I hold in my head.
The mummy's pleated gown
bandaging the wound of death.
And babies that grow inside you,
something you start and forget.

The blood spot my mother found in an egg
that had split, twinned in the shell,
stretching toward life.
She discarded it. I think it was
more than she wanted to know,
an accident, an interception.

Things seemed to come up
from the sewers in our house,
from the very sea, that we did not expect.

LESSON

That was Edena's mother,
whizzing the mixer. Eggs, butter,
pulled down into its vortex,
like a demonstration. Other
mothers whipped and whipped a spoon.
Her hair was neat in the nest
of a bun, maybe one feather of flour.
No cleaner kitchen. That kitchen,
a lab for the science of marriage.

When her father came home,
they sat at the bench while
Edena played him her lesson. His big hand
beat on the dark wood flank.
If she made a mistake a tic
fluttered her eye as he bellowed
the notes. Though she was good
it was clear he was better.

Then he'd call for dinner
and they said I could stay. After,
she washed while I dried. We came out
to watch, on the sofa, her father
cover her mother, moaning and touching,
rubbing away the differences.
More than once, this part
of the lesson. As often as I
was there, so they meant it to stick.

DRUGSTORE

It wouldn't
be stealing, exactly.
You'd have to think,
mine, outside
of myself, and hunch,
to be hidden, swinging
a carapace of embarrassment
up over your shoulders.

Shame at having a self,
of anyone knowing
you have a self.
I am. I want.

I'd be alone
or sometimes
an old man stood
beside me, wheeling
a little vacuum cleaner
of oxygen. In the mirror

Doc tapped the quiet
powder into capsules.
Girls said
if he turned, if
he caught you,
he grabbed you,
touched you anywhere
before you got away,

lipstick cupped in
your hand, your fist

dimming the shine. Lips
moving to that wet red.

While Doc bent, melted,
a man made of wax, even
the slur of his words.
Grinding and counting. Himself
a measure and a scale.

If he turned, if he saw
where you dissolve,
tuck in your hair,
chew away fingertips—

As when, sick, I'd wake,
the sun would find me,
stunned back again
into my body,

a throat that piped
medicine into a belly
and below, legs
stretching out,
the between that lay
between them.

SAND

Didn't I glimpse it
from the train

piled up in cones,
twitching pyramids,

its impossible colors, basalt
and flamingo,

look for it to cohere, almost
invisibly fly apart,

whisper or promise,
creep ahead that inch

into my life? Didn't
a monk draped in fire

blow through a wand,
directing it, painting a prayer

he later undid
with a wipe of his sleeve?

Didn't I find a way
myself to burrow in,

breasts and belly sink,
quake and settle?

MILITARY BALL

Somebody said something awful
or maybe they didn't. Love is such

a whitewash. I want to remember
what was said and if that leaning together

only meant to keep us standing.
The branches were waving, the shuddering

leaves. My breath shaken out
like rain out of trees. His damp palm

at my waist, steadying me. My cadet
and I, grass crushed between

our opposing toes. A moon drained the color
from my palest blue dress.

Music connected us. I remember the metronome's
hesitation, the skipped step in the waltz.

Sepal, I could just make out, and mottled leaf,
the straining fingers of the lily,

all the complications of the garden.
At dusk I watched the rabbits stiffen

while, far off, acrobats tumbled on the grass.
Their deftness, their silent

concentration. I felt his palm
molding the shape of my body.

Painted marionettes, we were,
disconnected figures on sticks.

Moon fingering silk. Warmth rose
from the grass. The dance, advance,

retreat, a bare spot worn into the earth.
He was right to wear the uniform of war.

BETROTHAL AT THE WELL

At a well, a maiden (*na'arah*)
is drawing water. A stranger arrives.
He is footsore, weary. The maiden,
hospitable, invites him home.
 The stranger has run away, he has
been driven away, he has come to seek
his fortune. He has come for her.
This she knows and doesn't know.
She hopes. It is why she is
so often at the well. The water
is her future. Her brother welcomes him,
"Come in, O blessed of the Lord,"
examines the stranger's gifts, nose ring
and bracelets, that already attach
the maiden to him. Not surprisingly,
the stranger asks for the maiden's hand.
Maybe not for himself, maybe he
is a servant, his master has sent him.
If so she has wasted that first look
with her heart. Could it be otherwise?
Behold: a manservant, in spite of his thirst.
A cipher, only meant to hold the place.
The covenant depends on it.

SLEEPING RATS DREAM OF THE MAZE

—a study of happiness and its effects

One group of women was told
to think of the best time of their lives,
and another, of the worst.
Then they all got flu shots.

No surprise who'd produce antibodies.
And yet, and yet. So many years,
so much to sift through,
                    (cutting and pasting, déjà vu).
Abuse, poverty, abandonment.
On the other hand,
love, paychecks, babies.

Didn't the researchers know,
the way a novel is about something
besides what happens, people's lives
are about something else too?

Skin the texture of shot silk,
a body that has gone on for years
without interference,
that might as well be inert matter,

suddenly all knobs and compartments,
recklessly flung open.

That there are days you can't
get up, pulling off the covers feels like
pulling off a bandage.

(Because the body has tricks. Tricks
and tricks. Not just the one breast
but, after all, both.)

Think back. Harm, unstoppable.
You looked to the moon. It couldn't
do anything, could it? It gave you
its blank stare, but still it made
a place to get away to, out of
the room where your life was.

Or think. Think. The flat water. Riding
in a car, alongside snow.
The fir trees. Someone's arms.
It's winter. You never believed you could
get warm enough.

SPIDER BITES

She dreams of someone,
imagining his anger, imagining
it as burning red circles

rise in relief, up
her leg, up her arm, leading
to the heart. The creature's
purple eyeshine, furry
cello body jumping,
the way sorry
jumps into her throat.

While she sleeps,
a log with a pulse.
But spiders are small,
inject only a small
jet of poison,
then escape on a strand of silk.

They'd shelter in her clothes,
in a folded towel, and bite
the way his profile
bites into white air. All belly,

what hides in her house,
what attaches to her,
that the night leaves,
that she must deserve.

CARIÑA

In Havana once, you walked the seawall
in the wind. Bleeding fuchsia lined the way
and sun and salt spray clung to you.
"*Cariña!*" you heard and blushing,
turned. Your young body, a catchall of praise.
More gullible, you were, than vain,
so eager for the praise of men, sifting it out
from an unknown language: cute, dear.

You've had to move that life aside
to make room for this one. Today,
you're here among chicory and confused grasses.
A bird calls, a sound like tinkling glass.
You see what you have longed to see,
so far absent from your life. Only
a miniature horse in a field. But the horn

grows out of your imagination. *Cariña.*
Dainty freak. The size of a sheep,
belly braced on short, tent-pole legs.
Mane, the mane is an emblem, a means
to swing up, on top of, away. The horn
you'd let nudge you to the end of the earth.

Cariña. It could be a cognate of
careening. Precarious. The way
a young woman might need to fight her way
out of a car or dark basement. For its size
you love the little horse. For the ground
it covers and doesn't want to leave.
The care it causes another creature to take
to step over or around, not trample it.

NOT TOO **IV**

LIGHT AND HEAT

> "I'd rather be a raindrop returned to the sea than a soul in
> hell."
> —*Doctor Faustus*

1.

The Mammogram

Each year, the same
X-ray. Silhouette of night.
Something mountain, something sky.
Then stars break through the dark transparency.
Calcifications, a trail

to cells the hormone feeds, not the usual, weak,
with their life sentence. Others,
fire-blackened trees death grows.

> (This was a way of saying it:
> *I was not a martyr, I was not a saint,*
> *but they pierced my breast*
> *with a needle and cut the rot away.*)

Visualize, someone says,
the color of earth or sky.
Green as water. Blue, like air.
Let it enter you, fill the shape
first of a foot, then leg, the torso.

2.

Treatment

The elevator sinks to that half-life
beneath cement, beneath lead.
The treatment unit.
 "You can go back now and change."
Oh, if you could.

In the waiting room, light and dark
clasp fingers like a Velásquez. You wait,
you contemplate your sins. On the table,
magazines thumbed back to pulp. Even the chair
beneath you, an evasion.

> *(Why I slumped where I sat: I was*
> *bowing to the world. Why I read:*
> *I would have been in anyone else's story.)*

An odd bird, Velásquez.
Solitary. A hawk. The way
he swooped down
on the contents of a room.
Sunlit or torchlit. Warren
or dwelling place. Empty or filled
with bright bodies. Human finery,
glazed vessels.

On the TV a chef whips and whips
the whites, leaning into them
his high, pleated hat.

Now he lights the brandy.

Here in your chest,
heat so intense if you could touch inside
you would pull back your hand.

3.

<u>Light</u>

       "Don't move.
We'll move you." A bounce. A child
on a horse.
You can't predict
how long it will take. Fifteen seconds.

Twenty-five.
The body gathers mass,
outside of time, outside of
Karmic advancement.

Salvage, they call it, saving you,
shining light through.
You are porcelain,
translucent as a teacup.

Addition modulo 12,
you subtract to know the time.
The thirteenth hour, one.
If you forget,
it comes around again.

      (I'd make a clock exactly backward, counter-
      clockwise: the way if it were up to me,
      it would go.)

4.

Heat

The sun at the edge. It falls.
Everyone advances, backlit red cutouts.

People walking dogs, a blood-red shadow
that runs along with them, upside down,
trying to get away.

> *(I am driving two cars, in two lanes*
> *separated by boxwood. Each in turn*
> *spontaneously combusts.)*

The demon of light, the demon of thunder,
instruments of education,
like the fiery cart you ride on.

> *(I lower and lower myself*
> *until I am flat,*
> *until I have no past, cast no shadow.)*

SMALL HOURS

In any park there's a crow, startled,
aiming for a tree where a little girl
hides her eyes and counts to 100
as everyone reaches cover. Time going,
the small voice keeping track. It could be me,
thinking and thinking of something.

Later, at home with her brothers and sisters,
all these strangers who move through the house,
the bathroom, the only room the father's
sure to recognize. Once a squirrel
dropped through the chimney into the whole
ruined civilization of the basement. Here,
I'm taking the squirrel's viewpoint.

It is better to live by this park than, say,
in Bhutan where there are no chimneys,
and the smoke goes out through
every open window. Anywhere though,
the body that has been opened
remains sealed with a language of scars.
At night I have the sense of being swept up
and contained in my bed
until the first of the world shows up,
half the silver bike handle, ivy flapping in the yard.

FOR LAURA

See where the earth shines,
pink-golden, trying
to attract you—so many
interruptions, though. A self
that comes between the selves:
"Weasel breath, white ice cream…"

Your voice catches
in the mesh of an unknown
language, each sound a sigh,
an indrawn breath. I want to know,
How are you? and a minute
from now, How are you?

I pinch away dead blossoms
from flowers on the sill,
so easy, walking the room
in a dance. See, space
is a container for the body.

Then I take the opal
of your hand, your hand,
that's still, most you. And think
of the cardinal, smashing
again and again against my window.
"Hitherto," he'd say, "Heretofore."
Either way, the same nostalgia.

56

RETURN TO WINTER

That day the starlings didn't eat.
That day was a sudden return
to winter. In the fields,
snow on a base of ice.

The birds couldn't bear
to set down except
on the clear face
of the road they remembered.

My husband leaned on the horn
the way you lean on a railing
until they lifted
before the unstoppable metal.

I pushed into the floorboard
as if I were doing the driving,
as if I could halt
the laws of physics,
while somewhere, my brother's chest
rose and sunk and rose.

So much you take for granted,
like going to sleep in spring
that you will wake in spring.
That the blossoms were right
to push out, there was
no contradiction.

But when we hit the slick
and slammed hard against
our own forward motion,

the roadbank spun
and the orchard of stunted trees
that had just begun to soften.

MR. C. BRINGS HIS CAT TO SCHOOL

Imagine, another living thing,
unpredictable as ourselves
in the steady, dim light of school.
And the kids we were, we didn't have pets.
Some of us slept
in tunnels under the subway.

Keisha put out a hand, finding
the nap of it, until a spark
warned her off. Oh, she said.
Then everyone wanted to touch.
Oh. Ooh. Some held their breath.

Black with the white patches.
It looked as if parts might be missing.
A boy, a little rough, put his face
up against its face, but then he laughed.
No one wanted to hurt it.

What makes her a cat? Mr. C. asked,
not a dog or a person?
We thought about that. Well,
her ears stand up. Why? To hear better.
And she had the sharp teeth and nails
like tiny swords to protect her.

Of course, we wanted her back.
Once, we asked, and no,
she couldn't come, it was her stomach.

Later, she wasn't seeing
so good. Something had grown

inside her brain, Mr. C. thought.
Tyrell said, they should just
cut it out. But no, they couldn't,
it was too big.

         Always, How's
your cat? we remembered to ask.
By now, his head shaved,
there was something red like
a map of the country
we were studying in geography

stretching back from Mr. C.'s forehead.
And after, all of us were spared
asking and answering.
After, it was the end of the term.

TWENTY-THREE WEEKS

Before skin or breath.
That baby, plucked out,
less than a baby,
blood nearly to the surface
like a deep flush. Elbow to heel,
the size of a bat. A bell

calls doctors and nurses
from their stations to this show
of life: wide movements,
womb-swimming breaststroke.
Then the whole obstetrical team
is circling, keeping him going.
Machines jiggle the tiny heart,
paper lungs beaten thin,
open to air.

        At this point dawn
is just a filter against dark, a chance,
not a promise. Those pink carnations
in the mother's room
that yesterday were sleepy and closed
have now begun to shout.

The wish of the mother
attaches itself
to the father's wish, "Live!"
Imagine a melon, swollen fruit
that smells of earth, a sweet moist cave,
a hole in the ground
where it hid and ripened,
leaving a vine for a trail, a gold fly

on a leaf. Live. One step, then another,
bright sun and protecting trees.
Cat, dog, grass, you won't know where
to look. Grasp. Claw.

But already he's learned
that desire is suffering, that birth
is desire thrust into life. Soon even
the doctors and nurses
are willing to let go.

Not to be born.
To have bypassed this, formed no
attachment to the world.
Like rain or wind,
to have only been waved through.

NOTO **V**

HYPOTHETICAL ARCHITECTURE

Without us a house
is flighty, insubstantial.

It drifts off, leaving the children
standing at the bus stop
or drapes itself
with whatever else we remove
over clotheslines.

We close the door
and don't know
what becomes of it. The empty bedroom,
where your head inched
in and out of your sleep
like a turtle's.

Windows narrowing the focus
so that the only view
falls onto the opposite house

where now Tess and Charlie
have returned from a long trip.
She, planting a middle finger
up to the first joint
after every petunia in the window box.

Oh, to leave your house
fluttering in the wind like the bedclothes.
To walk a finger
over the whole earth like that
and come back, dipping into
your own dirt again,
letting it reassure you.

IN ITALY

There, you have cold, have hunger,
keep them in your possession, not
subsumed. The way travel is,
like a dream where you live
on the reverse side of the street.

You feel evident, a misplaced object.
Fragile as what breaks away
from ancient statues, nose, arms, the penis.

And sometimes there, the present
has a future idea. A finger
on the throat as words form
that you are impatient to know,

that you never need once you've left.
Meanwhile, you watch nuns
mount ladders in an olive grove
like vowels in a diphthong, straightening.

HANDLE

I forget a name. I forget it because
it's useless. At best, it carries its burden
like some poor beaten animal,
an eyebrow, the shape of a mouth,
a bridge shadowing water
weighted down by the color of stones.
At best, it floats a memory to safety
as a tabletop will a person in a flood.

A name is a handle. On an urn,
on a door, on a black lacquered chest
with chinoiserie flowers
where jades are kept, pendants and rings,
tiny green cups netted with age.
The handles point out at you,
they grow into your hands.

But does a name change the mouth's lash,
the circumflexive eyebrow?
The jolt as your racing cab
halts at the edge of a tar-stained pier
while a boat is just pushing off
to lost islands? Salt taste
of the Coke you hold to your cheek
to cool your haste and disappointment.

A STORY

As in my dreams
where I can see only
over someone's shoulder
or in a bookcase
through a gap between books,

I spot on the street a woman's
beautiful, impervious face
like a China plate. She is
talking to air. "That's

the end," she says.
"That's all there is, that's
my story." I'm sorry
to have missed the good part,
hovering over us like vapor.

What drops at her feet?—
a bird, a leaf, a candywrapper,
something from the world.
I know that even without that
encouragement, she would go on.

Her past, like the Prairie
before dark, wild cosmos
and dense, high weeds, never cut.
She can't help herself.

Think of those people who call
middle of the night from
the impossibly far reaches of an old
friendship, new acquaintance.

They've read in your face,
"I'm here." The practice
and circumspection of the holy man
who has stood
on one foot for eight years.

It isn't you they want,
voice thinning out to ether,
only access to the entrails
of the divine animal.

NOTO

She is thinking that something must
have happened in the unraveling
of her life, even today, something.

That why, if we come into this naked,
we should go out in our best,
the body all this time, gathering
necessities like a grocery cart.

And that probably, each time
as a child she waved her hand
in the teacher's face, desperate,
"Save me!" is what she was saying.

Which reminds her of this movie,
L'Avventura, where they go to a town
called Noto to look for, or not to,
a woman who has vanished. Or

of those beatings, the arm falling,
no longer part of a person
but a force of nature. Even when

she'd hear the thunder's shouts
and rain spread over roofs
and into the groove of leaves

it would be the sound of those blows
reverberating, narrowing
the margin between the sky
and ground.

A tiny rain, any other,
just her little finger's worth of rain,

the shrink once telling her
that the first word out of her mouth
in the morning should be a scream,
the two ends of her voice, reattaching.

PASSAGE

Canada geese, always ahead,
rope ladder swinging over,
touching down. Their sobs.

I'd have gone, then. Someplace,
not knowing. I'd felt the pull,
how my heart could float to safety.

What we gave them we thought
they wanted, water, bread, mild winters.
Time, not the timeless wild.

Think of them then, mastering
the exigencies of flight and uncertainty.
Now they ask us, they beg.

THE PINES: A JOURNAL

—Millay Arts Colony

A manse, the word for it,
a grand private mansion,
and yet it seems to me
the last of civilization,
where it is just pinned to the trees.

A white housefront,
a right angle
against feathery dark. Of course,

you can't escape its beauty.
It slashes through
like the best knife.

★

I am afraid for that shack
by the side of the road.
People poor in that way, exposed
to winter. Snow outside
each time they'd look.

But this summer night,
moths flatten against the glass
like still-hungry ghosts.
A gloating moon marbles the trees,
makes a graveyard of day.

★

I wake to such clear definition,
sun scattered along the ground.
I feel the press of the mountains.

All day a scent of crushed berries,
so few words spoken,
I'll remember each one.

★

For hours I stare out
at those trees, not
as a painter does, not to remember,
only to get past them.

★

Patterned silk,
the mower's circles in the grass.
I walk to the ruined pool,
sprays of insects at its surface,
stone cherubs nodding.

The outdoor bar, jagged wood,
curtained by ferns.
I imagine a shimmer of party guests.
Lupine in the raised
flower beds and columbine,
wheel moving within wheel.
All of us waiting for dark,
for the blur of anything
we can still make out.

★

Wind searches the low branches,
vibrato of desire.

Think of them,
whole afternoons, making love,
one threaded into the other,
wild shadows sweeping over them.
The wolf comes out
in your face then,
there's such desperation.
Oh, that poor excuse, that human body.

★

I follow a gravel path
until moss softens my footsteps.
Approach at last
the cul de sac at the gravesites.
A breeze or an insect
just lifts the hair from my forehead.

Then what a scrambling
and clutching of branches,
while I remark to myself
the steady spires of trillium.

Operatic, billowing voices,
wind leavening the trees, storm cloud
like an arm raised behind me.

★

The thunder god, the axe.
Once a tornado bit away
the top third of the trees

in their long watch by the drive.
A stray dog got in then
and ran for the cellar.

★

In the barn, thin sunlight
criss-crosses a weft of spider web.
Damp comes in, the moist outdoors
on each breath I take.

★

This is what a story does, lay crumbs
along a path.

        In the thickest part
of the pines, all that remains
is a rust colored fundament of needles
where nothing grows.

HYPERSTARTLE

On 16th St.
a teenager's loud falsetto
wavers over
an old gospel song,
"Take away the sickness
and the pa-ai-aine—"
He makes it, maybe it is,
so many words.
Those red lights
at his shoulder,
only geraniums
in a window box.

But I am startled,
stopped in mid-step.
A snake could do it,
or fireworks
starting up again and again.
Even uncommon beauty.
A startle requires
immediate attention.
Your mouth drops open,
your hand rises up
as if to wave.

A startle
is like an angel rising
from a river of fire,
brief in its life
like an insect.
When I was born,
one wiped away what I knew

with his thumb,
pressing a groove
into my upper lip,
stunning me to silence.

CHOSEN

So where was Moses all this time?
No longer slaves,
they forgot why they were waiting.

Now they were like nearly everybody,
most of their lives spent
with things moved
just to the right or left of them,
just out of reach.

Bright finches flew past,
opening like fists.

Did they think of themselves
as people who stood ready
to enter a covenant with God?
It was too hard, like the dead
trying to explain to those still living.

And where was this Moses
taking them? Weren't there
graves enough in Egypt?

They threw their bracelets and earrings
into the fire. That glint of eternity
like a magician's trick
at their ears. A quick god
they fashioned themselves.

Moses knew that
if you interfere with people
they become your responsibility for life.

Yet he broke the gold calf,
likewise, the stone tablets.

And God came like an eagle
and lifted him out of the mountain,
lending him credibility.

And they starved and ate
and got sick and recovered
and lived and died,
in other words, they suffered.
Until, Give us a God
without limits, they begged,
a God to depend on.

SILENT RETREAT

1.

So interesting, Rhoda says.
No talking, even at supper.
You eat. You meditate.
Your chewing becomes
a kind of chant. Sometimes
you start to open your mouth
to say something, then remember,
swallowing your words.
It's so still you think you hear
the food pass through the body.
That is a funny thing, and you want
to laugh. After supper, there's
a throb of treefrogs everywhere.
And sometimes at night a bat
sweeps the window like a fist in a glove,
picking off moths. Then, in the time
before sleep, though no one is calling,
the air grows heavy with your name.

2.

Nothing in myself speaks
to me anymore. I want
to be distracted from myself
so I call for the world to move closer.

Moon, I say,
so full of yourself,
like the ball of the soul
bouncing against the words.

But what I say
is only a part of what I mean.
Socrates is right. The alphabet
helps you forget, like
a long dream.

3.

At a party once,
I lost my voice. No words,
just a ping at my lips
like bits breaking off frozen.

I gestured with my hands.
People thought this was
a pantomime. Where was
my horn, my curly wig?

At last, I took up a pencil and pad.
I got at it, elaborated,
until my writing fingers cramped
as if they were stanching a wound.

SALTMEN OF TIBET

As the harvesters approach the salt lake,
they change the pitch of their voices.

The words they speak are like their own words
written upside down and backward.

They must not fart or fornicate on the journey.
No one who does can return

to the village, where the women
and barking dogs wait to greet them.

Salt is a jealous goddess. If a woman were
to go to the lake the salt would disappear,

even if a woman were only to turn
her face in its direction.

The men make a new world
to one another, the world of salt.

One is *margen*, old mother, another, *pargen*,
old father. The others, their loved sons.

They go from tent to tent,
eating dumpling soup and discussing things.

At night the lord of animals
watches over the good yak.

It is a strong and versatile beast
that will eat sand where there is no grass.

Its intestines can twist, causing it
to grow ill and die. But it goes forward

to where the lake starts, and returns
in silence with its load of salt.

THE FIRST TIME

Last night for the first time
I dreamed I died.
But I went on living after
to see what this meant to the world.

For a while the shade
did not advance,
the sun didn't retreat.
It was permanent afternoon.

A train arrived at a station
and all the stunning scenery fled
that the whole way
had been rubbing up against it.

Somewhere a man laid out
a game of solitaire
on a wrought-iron table.
Just his hands, what I saw,
and the cards.

And everywhere people stood or walked,
separate, upended, carrying
as they do
that cross in the shape
of their bodies.

There was a brittleness in the leaves,
the summer stiffening.
My eyes closed
in my dream, and an hour passed

very fast in sleep. I woke
at the slap of pigeon wings
against the red-tiled roofs.
The shade came then, and it gave
a shape to everything.
I could see I wasn't alone. Other spirits
crouched in the mountains.

Soon the same stars I remembered
would burn, they'd be
as persistent. And that was that,
night overtaking day, autumn, summer,
shadow falling over
the face of the apple.

from The Dog's Heart (2002)

NIGHT BLOOMING CEREUS

I push away a nearly
irresistible sleep
to follow her in her pale gown.

Our flashlights braid
wide swathes of green on the lawn.

"We plant it," he'd said
"then wait for it to surprise us."
She had outwaited him.

Then one day, a tiny pearl appeared
in the notch of a leaf. And now,
oh, most astonishing,
the universe poised
between expansion and collapse,
above a half-moon, rocking,
we stumble into its scent,
which, like memory itself, seems
to release heat, to increase disorder.

Light separates the petals.
We watch the oily, white socket dilate
as something stabs out
like an infant's fist, and is held,
throbbing, in the present.

FERAL GIRL FOUND IN A SUBURBAN HOUSE

We know her by the two perfect
sets of teeth, that grew in
like a shark's, one within the other.
Or when we speak, the way she stares
at a spot just over our shoulders
that seems more forgiving.

She is small and bent, as if
prepared to spring. She'd been strapped
for hours to the potty chair,
a creature like herself, hugging
the ground. The gods she invented
must have squatted on their haunches.

She doesn't feel heat. Her skin
is moist and cool like something
taken from a wood. Locked in her closet,
she played with two plastic raincoats,
red and green, and learned
to move sidewise like a beam of light.
She came out spitting and scratching.

Out of the noise surrounding her,
birds, lawn mowers, thunder,
she pulled the syllables
for food, one long vowel. For no,
a hiss that gives nothing away.

THIEF

It is daylight still
but I have gotten inside, who knows,
the way the worm
gets into the dog's heart.
These houses,
I tell you, are heartless.
They seem all light and air,
that glass, a skin
as fragile as an animal's.

But upstairs
a man may be lying on his back
until a gulp or start wakes him.
How long I stand listening
for that tread I fear
from the floor above.

I've stepped into
a room all reds and greens,
the soft, sharp points of Persian rugs,
of mohair furniture
I rub myself against.
I hold a bone china box
up to the light and a lovely,
calm emptiness
opens before me.

I walk through a doorway without doors
then another, taking up
knick-knacks pining for use
and breathe on them.
No one for years has been so kind.

From here I look out and see
the last of the sun bond
to the gingko leaves, that gilding
so like astonishment.
Then a wind stirs the branches.
I am aware of this circling
from the ground up.
Inside me too there's something
that can't stop.

Even now a woman
may be leading an aproned boy
back with her groceries.
I feel that swivel of my neck
to the outside door, to the place
where the action happens.
Oh, what do I steal
but a little of her happiness?

I could test each wall
for another way out.
But the dog is in the yard,
big Doberman with his awaiting bark.
Also, the roll of a high, dark hedge.
Surely, though, I am safe. Surely
I can open the refrigerator yet
and in a cloud of light
drink deeply the milk
of whoever lives here.

THE RUIN

1.

Is the ruin a shell or a skeleton?

We passed the smoking banners
of the nuclear plant going into its country.
Nuns and pilgrims, soldiers also
have been travelers here.

2.

In the photo the ruin
seems all there is. Really, though,
a rope and empty space
are needed to set it apart. It is as if
they'd wanted to scratch this one place
clear of all connection. Otherwise
it would be just the past continuing.

3.

The ruin's rectangles and perfect circles
seem a sequence of development and decline.

Don't you remember the road here?
At first, like anywhere,
a white church, a river curling.
Then quarry, dam, mill, every stop

a power point, which is clear in the names
our fathers gave them, something
they meant to tell us.

4.

Perhaps the ruin is a tool to measure
the transit of heavenly bodies,
for we know that its main axis
aligns with the sun on the longest day.

Therefore, the sky is the real structure here.
The ruin is only broken teeth in its mouth.
Long ago, the sun rose

in the niche between rocks, as it does now.
If it rose to the left, there would be
a rainy season, to the right,
a season for hunting and war.

5.

The ruin parts the grass
as the grass once broke through stone
for the long time when people
forgot how to live in cities.

6.

We must pay an admission fee.
At sunset red flares rise in a spray
again from the ruin's depths. Should we applaud?

SARAJEVO

Play on,
Vedran Smailovic,
cellist for the opera.
Others have stopped practicing.
They say, "For What? We live like rats,"

while for these 22 days
you put on formal dress
and sit outside the bakery
to play Albinoni's *Adagio*,
that series of beginnings
which rises and rises
out of itself.

The music's dark wings
must close over you
to keep you safe,
as shells pierce
the surrounding air,
fire answering fire.

You play once
for each
of the 22 hungry citizens
killed by mortar blast
as they stood here in line for bread.

FLOATER

I had to push myself
away from the window to watch TV,
even the Democratic convention,
police marching behind shields
like gladiators.

And all that summer, I was mindful
of what I was using up,
water, paper, daylight, even the thoughts
going through my head.

Paula had lent me her apartment.
She'd gone to the country,
an abandoned farm where hunters wintered—
I imagined bats wheeling around
the dome of a barn, and below,
children on bikes, echoing their shrieks.
Later, parents who read bedtime stories
very fast, racing sleep.

I was here because I had walked out of my life.
I was a floater,
like those first-year birds
who wait for the chance to swoop down
and quickly replace the territorial bird.

There were plants to water,
but I could leave them, Paula said.
Dark green succulents
that stuck up like thumbs.
The tables were topped
with collections of shells and stones.

But so little could I find
in this place that I wanted,
string and fasteners in a kitchen drawer,
a melonballer. I ate

in the coffee shop around the corner
where cakes were left in a glass pillar,
their icings hardening like paint.

THE CURRENT

Two swans, affixed
to the mirror of the river,
to each other. Until one,
in widening circles,
copies the loose cast
of the hawk above. He rocks
and dips. A separation
of feathers. One wing
acts as a rudder.

He goes only as far
as an emerging shoal, but she
comes effortlessly forth
to meet him. What moves her
is what moves the water:
the current. What is happening
right now. The drift. The wind.
The pull of him.

SPRING TWILIGHT

The ferns uncoiling,
the fir trees shooting out
their first bright extensions,
you go off to clear a path
between living trees.
It is almost dusk.
I watch the sun slide off
the tips of leaves.
Then a wind is circling
bushes and weeds.
Even the trees start to move
in wide figure eights.
Maybe by now you've reached
the dump at the edge of the road,
that mountain of decay
smelling of crushed plaster and rust,
where dead sunflowers
duel with iron rods. I can hear
the chastening cry of the crows.
Then a tanager plummets like
a drop of blood.

SKIRT

It wasn't meant to happen. Like a knife
that slips through bread
and into the first joint of your finger.
I was a woman in a dress and pearls.
My footing sure, the front of me
so carefully put together.

And this was a block of firmly closed doors.
Lawn after lawn, the green rectangles
going on forever. No razor wire
or stagnant gutters anywhere. No one ahead,
but one man moving toward me.

It was a summer afternoon. I'd been looking away,
studying the dead air beside me. We should
have passed like two bars of light,
but he grabbed my skirt and threw it
up over my shoulders.

Then, like a scene in a painting
that takes place half in the sky, I am where I am
and at the same time, locked out of my body.

I must have known this was nothing,
that worse went on within those walls.

That smear of sound, only a record started wrong,
something torn. For I stood there, hushed,
like a tree with fire at its heart.

SECRET MEANINGS

Sometimes our houses shake in the night.
It may be thieves loosening the copper down spouts—

we are not far from boarded-up windows
you could beat and beat your fists against—

and sometimes, too, we hear sirens though
only a single laugh is left to glow in the dark.

Or that odd bird bleats its same, repeating signal
like a voice abstracted from a dialogue.

Not the bird whose song starts as flat statement,
then dips and flounders into melody. No.

That one would stop when the dark became impenetrable.
This bird goes on, a sound that is like white petals

fleeing from yard to yard. We can never find him,
though the moon, too, is an ardent hunter.

MERRY-GO-ROUND

Thus I become conscious
of the objects of the world,
little girl on a rusty
mechanical horse. Red buds
are sprouting on the trees
above my life. Days at school
I sit behind my desk, behind
a whole wooden consciousness,
waiting for the merry-go-round.

It is made from the parts
or ideas of animals. With a jerk,
they are hammering. So swift,
yet so still. That great, wheeling darkness
is the shadow of the canopy.
This is its barn, this is its stable.

Gilding and colored glass,
mirrors that flash back light.
Even plaster is important.
I see that the world
is not flesh, not straw. Not anything
that I find easily, loose
in the dirt. Oh, sculptured island,
no one has questioned your right

to turn, ever. Yet sometimes,
I would like my mind to let
the animals go, let them move off
through darkening trees
as the fireflies the riders
throw over their shoulders explode.

THE CLEANSING

When a knife meant for dairy
was used mistakenly to cut meat,
hadn't my mother, the same night,

plunged it into the ground*
to cleanse it, sure that the dirt
had power, that it forgave?

And what would they make of this,
those people who lived beside us?

Really, our houses were thrown
against one another, though
in my dreams there might be
a moon and a tree between us
or a silhouette of porch steps.

The boy once stood in his window,
taking off his pajamas
for me to see. The moonlight
fell over his front like quarters.

He'd beat me up as we walked
from school. No one could make him stop.
Our families no longer spoke.

This was hard, like
swallowing knives. We'd sit
on adjoining patios,
metal chairs whining, and look away.
We might have been set out in a desert.

*ritual connected to Orthodox Jewish dietary law

Once I said so loud, I must have
meant them to hear, that what
was good about the A-bomb is,
we would all die at once.

MINISTRY TO THE JEWS

We were in a park. I'd left
my mother on a bench
beside her friend, the Christian
missionary.—Do I need to speak
of my mother's loneliness,
of her hunger for anyone's word?—

This was a stiff lady who smelled
of dead flowers. She had been
to China and Africa. I had from her
a small, crocheted cross
that I kept with my handkerchiefs.

I went off alone
to where the trees were thickest.
Leaves moved in the wind
like tinkling ornaments
and here and there embroidered tiny corpses
hung from spider webs.
On my finger was that ruby ring, my birthstone.

I watched a squirrel climb down head first
from the nearest tree, his eye
shining into my eye. To think,
he ate out of my hand!

Then, so quick I wasn't frightened,
he'd fastened his teeth
around the red stone and bit, hard.

A small, savage act.
Yet he didn't even break the skin,
leaving only these tiny marks in the gold
that have become part of the design.

THE SPOT

The spring my father died,
when I came to believe that everyone
was mortal, I found a spot at the back of my leg,
jagged and dark, that held on like a tick.
I waited for it to grow into a cancer.
First blemish, I thought, in a spoiling fruit.
So small, and yet a mark, a certainty.

I'd been in Egypt, studying the past.
One day, a colossus lay before me in sand
as if it had just fallen across my path.
A cart driver was taking me along the desert
to a buttery or a pottery, he might even
have been saying, leprosary. He couldn't
be stopped. We came at last to a Coptic church
where he showed me signs drawn
in old copy books, a blue-tiled emptiness.

I became aware of the spot as I climbed
up to my place in a vast arena.
I was looking down behind me at small,
scattering figures. The performance,
a circus or spectacle, just about to begin.

NECESSITY

I lived for the first time
away from home two floors up
from a furrier and just above
a Greek family
where a sister killed her brother.

Some Saturdays a deaf man
went from door to door selling needles.
And I thought, "Yes.
What a quiet activity it is,
to sew." I too lived
without the bewitchment of speech.
Even the sound of rain stunned me.
So I trembled to hear
the wretched mother keening.

Slowly, I filled up my small room—
the years at home had starved me
of myself. To say I was happy
is not exact. More,
like someone who agrees
to her own sacrifice or exile,
that it was necessary.

Night after night
the woman's wails rose up
through the floorboards.
I imagined her in black, rent clothes
with her double sorrow,
grief rising and falling back.
I imagined
that terrible rocking.

DIABOLE

You know how night shuts down everything,
and it is only the moon that stands there,
beckoning?

       Well, I am thinking of
Rembrandt's dark interiors, how he pulls
the person out of the shadows. "Woman with Pink,"
for instance. She is holding a flower before her
as if to light her way into the world.

Or of vampires, who can only live, if that
is what they do, at night—collectors
of loss, my friend, an expert, calls them,
dirt from the homeland, one or two

bartered Botticellis. Theirs is strictly
a literary existence, no roots, she'd say,
in the collective unconscious. That is why
they are beloved, creatures of longing,
as we are, for what has never been.

I did not go to the high school reunion.
Twenty known deaths so far.
Even our crewcut class president
who led cheers in white bucks,
raving away the dark.

       Sometimes now,
there's the same impatient rain
I remember from that time, with a brilliant sun
to follow, radiance behind everything,
like a view glimpsed in a rearview mirror.

Tonight, eating these half-withered, negative
little plums, the end of their season,
I am listening to Bach's *Partita* for solo violin.
Imagine the instrument,
pouring out its heart alone like that.

from DAMAGES (1996)

PHOBIA

Because from the tour bus
I could not hear even the cries of vendors,
only staring out at brilliant tinware
and pottery set up on stands,
the occasional geranium unfurling
on the windowsill of crumbling,
whitewashed housefronts,
how should I know when not to look?

As the bus turns I witness
that starburst of frazzled flight,
a startled chicken scratching up dirt.
The comb and wattles are like
congealed blood. Behind the glass
my limbs are jerking in response.
I feel the sharp beak, the talons digging in.

In my mouth is a taste
of decomposing food. My husband
can't think what to do. I am a person
in a dream. And yet he sees
the sickness and the sweat are real.
He reaches out his hand as my mother
must once have reached out hers,
a link to any possibility.

My mother who so loved birds,
who chattered to them as she chattered
to me. I fetched her a crippled starling once,
frail and speckled, a rival heartbeat
in my hand. She fed it milk-soaked bread
till it was black and sleek, till it would fly up

and sit, a dark sign, on her shoulder.
But that is not what troubled me. It was only
the wings beating like something
that will not be settled in life.

At the hotel that night, still feverish,
I draw between my thumb and middle finger
the cool satin ribbon that trims
the pillow slip. I press my wedding band
to my mouth as if to quiet it, but overhead
the whir of the ceiling fan
wrenches me back again and again from sleep
with its frantic wings.

THE MAD SCHOOL

1.

We teachers boost ourselves
up onto the low stone wall, our backs
to the outside. Someone has scattered
cow bones in the grass. It's how
these children learn, stumbling
across their lessons. Thus Frances,
dropping to the ground, discovers slugs.
A light of beautiful emptiness
comes into her face. Everyone kneels
to help her separate the wet dead dirt
from the live. We set them like small,
shivering mouths into an aquarium
with stones and flags of grass
and bring it in. I never see them move again.

Inside, I press my hand down hard
against the open book and read aloud,
or else just stare with them
through the windows' white-paned cells.
They are trying to hold still.
All it takes is a bell or a voice sounding out
the syllables of words—just the sun
blundering into the room, and soon Irene,
dwarfed and stoic as a fireplug,
begins to sob. Books, blocks, phantoms
are flung into the air. We move fast,
the aide and I, subduing. Once I have to sit on
the small, offending body. Once I sprain my back.

2.

All year I balance on the stone wall,
heels splintering mica. And then it's spring.
The skin splits on a bucket of sour creek water
I'd have turned out in the hallway sink.
A thin, unexpected thing, the new frog leaps.
The children, too, are growing.
But they are asymmetrical in their growth
like trees on a hill that the wind
blows only one way. I walk among them,
watch any one of them, watch the fingers
bend back tensely against what they want to do.
Watch Saul, in the hooded shirt, fierce and delicate
as a fallen angel, far off dragging trash cans
onto the train tracks, waiting for the accident.
Sometimes we take our classes swimming.
What it must mean to them
to leave the stone shoulders of the pool,
trusting to nothing, all their voices
all at once clawing at air.
I can only wade in up to my thighs and stop.

WHITE HEIFER

The night before my cousin Esther died
my mother dreamt of a white heifer.
There was no twisted metal
in her dream, no back seat
from which to lead the calf to safety.
My mother was pregnant with me then.
I was an eyelash on the back of her hand
that wouldn't blow away, not the favored girl.
She'd never have her back, not even
in the wish of a name. She spoke of her
from the dim doorway of my room,
nearly stumbling over the loss,
like a leg she could not touch down on.
I was saying my prayers, one after another
as if undoing buttons.
She stood in her nightgown, wringing her hands
that glistened with rose-scented cream.
I knew by then that this was how
she got her information,
so much of her life spent
in the shell of a dream.
Then she went to take her place
in the twin bed beside my father's
where he lay, sweat darkening his sheets.
And we slept like voyagers in boats,
they in front, that much
farther along than I.

AMUSEMENT PARK

When the man grips her arm
at Willow Grove Amusement Park,
it will be half a caress.
He will rub his fingers
along the inside of her wrist,
skin so delicate, so seldom touched
it seems unfamiliar even to her.

She and her friend are twelve
and loose as dimes in the world.
They are not themselves.
At the white, ornate gates
they have slid the smiles of grown women
in Tangee across their faces.

The park is wide and dusty.
They make their way through it,
roller coaster, rocket, flying cars.
Ride after ride lifts them
to where the sun breaks
over their tiny remembered earth,
drops them closer than they can stand to it.

Then the cricket that's her pulse
exposes itself, the beat of her own heart.

The two men have coaxed them
toward the trees, all four laced together
in the shadow of leaves. She has
been waiting all her life
for something to touch her. How then
is she able to pull herself loose
from that hand, so urgent, so particular?

118

THEIR HOUSE

They've built an understanding
with their pillars and 2x4s
and the crushed stone that goes into cement,
a way of cutting the dark to fit.
Moths flicker on the shiny, lit surfaces.
There is a border of red and white tulips
and impetuous birds sing. She learns to cook
such things as floating island.
He calls it eggs in snow.

They watch the wind
catch up the narrow yellow leaves
and listen for the knuckle-cracking thunder.
Then great stones begin to roll.
Rain falls. On the side of the woods
it falls again just for them
from the trees, gladly repeating itself.

But one day he notices an orange fungus
twisting over a tree stump.
It reminds him of his childhood, stiff and unreal.
And at night something flings bark and acorns
at the door. The pool,
green with algae, is sinking out of sight.
They forget the bright tanager,
its one note sucked through a straw.
Then no step in her garden
makes anything grow. Then theirs
is not a ship sailing with the wind
but a house with its chimney blown away.

When they leave, boards are knocking,
swollen out of place. Raccoons scratch
in the attic. It is hot and moist
under the rubble of their lives,
ideal conditions for growing. That summer
new owners are moving themselves in.
Younger, quicker. You can see
the sweat on their foreheads.
The woman in her flip-flops shoots ahead.
What does she carry in her arms? Ah,
she is hurrying in to feed their enormous baby.

SELF-EXAMINATION

He might be tethered
like an animal, kept from where
he wants to be. A big man,
nearing sixty. He sits and sweats,
though the room is air-conditioned.
His mouth a little open, he is reading
the sign on the door marked Radiology.
He is half up to go after her,

thinking of this life
of hers. The lapses in the love—
his love—which cushions it.
The mutilating surgery and drugs
that sting the organism so it
draws back into itself, counterforce
to the disease. Whatever she has suffered
away from him in other rooms.

I pass easily where he
is not allowed. Like her, I'm chilled
in my thin gown. There is
a fineness, a definiteness
to her face. This beauty
is her own decision. A TV screen
plays a loop of film, women circling
their breasts with their fingertips,
women staring into a mirror.

A foam-rubber breast is lying
on a table. Each of us takes it
in turn, like a lump of dough
we must knead smooth. Something solid

stops me. Unyielding, jewel-hard, a pebble
in this mud. Such seeds grow.

I touch the hollow between
my breasts, this emptiness
that is in me a sign of want.
I look at our still-dressed hands.
Watches, rings. What do they have
to do with us?—madly flashing in the light.

RUSH HOUR

Odd, the baby's scabbed face peeking over
the woman's shoulder. The little girl
at her side with her arm in a cast,
wearing a plaid taffeta party dress.
The woman herself who is in shorts and sunglasses
among commuters in the underground station. Her body
that sags and tenses at the same time.

The little girl has not once moved
to touch her or to be touched.
Even on the train, she never turns and says,
"Mommy." Sunlight bobs over her blond head
inclining toward the window. The baby
is excited now. "Loo, loo, loo, loo,"
he calls, a wet crescendo. "He's pulling
my hair," the little girl at last cries out.
A kind man comes up the aisle to see
the baby. He stares at those rosettes of blood
and wants to know what's wrong with him.
The woman says a dog bit him. "It must have been
a big dog, then." "Oh, no. A neighbor's little dog."
The man says, "I hope they put that dog to sleep."
The woman is nearly pleading. "It was an accident. He didn't
mean to do it." The conductor, taking tickets,

asks the little girl how she broke her arm.
But the child looks out to the big, shaded houses.
The woman says, "She doesn't like to talk
about that." No one has seen what is behind.
her own dark glasses. She pulls the children to her.
Maybe she is thinking of the arm raised over them,
its motion that would begin like a blessing.

NEEDLEWORK

Sometimes fate takes
a needle's path through cloth,
looping in and out,
retracing its own stitches,
twisting like a serpent.

In a Moorish seraglio
at Tordesillas, later a convent,
Phillippe, le Bel, kept one woman only,
Juana, his wife, Juana, la Loca,
in a cell with no windows
for forty-nine years.

Daughter of Ferdinand and Isabella,
mother of the Emperor Charles V,
she never stood beneath
the throne room's coffered ceiling,
never drew through her fingers
Phillippe's gift, red-violet tapestries
stiffened with gold.

Here one day Pedro the Cruel
would install his young mistress
and their daughter begin
the long chain of white-robed nuns.

Thyme climbed the hillside then,
as it does now. Sparrows flitted in dust,
scattering anywhere fear sent them.
Within her stone walls
Juana walked off from herself
into flowers and ferns,
past statues with their mouths open.

Each day was a union of light and sense,
her needle stammering through cloth
as trumpet vines vied for her attention
with the bright eyes
in the butterfly's orange wings.

THE SPELL

How tired I was, and I slept
from my twelfth birthday
until I was nearly eighteen.
A hot, rosy sleep, punctuated
by menstrual blood.

The booty of dreams,
the plaid silk dress that I loved,
and perfume bottles
won for my drawings
of long-haired dogs.

I could not have heard
the summer-loud insects
pluck at the screens
or the gathering of rain
as others did and been afraid.

The thin light of the house
shone in my eyes
but did not wake me.

I climbed to a room
papered with princesses.
There I lay down where birds slept
and fish, and the very crumbs
that could have told the way
out of the wilderness of sleep

slept. Sometime I rose
and left this cave of dark,
going out into the true dark
of the streets, of a boy's arms.

126

How had it planted itself
in my cells, this sleep?
Settling over me as snow settles
over mountains and winter rivers.
As my heavy knee-length hair
had settled over me
when I was a child.

GOODWIFE PLAYING THE VIRGINALS

—after a painting by de Witte

The woman's hands are hungry birds.
Here is their breakfast of music.

In the cabin bed her lover lies,
listening. The plucked notes scatter
along the keyboard of his spine.

A mirror returns the room to her,
velvets, red sashes, an earthenware jug.
The small dog, signaling fidelity.

Then a staccato of rectangles.
Who has upset these boxes
of sunlight on the floor?

One by one the ordered rooms open,
each staring into another's face.

Far off, a housemaid sweeps
at the speck in her mind.

Useless now, the man's sword
slung across a chair. The true scourge
is the broom on its hinge,
the maid's stout shoulder.

The man is trapped by the open door.

SPORTS PHOTOGRAPHER

—*for Jim Drake*

As a young man he ran. He knew
that the slapping of feet
is a natural language to the earth.
Then, in a sprint, his knee turned in.

After that, it was his eye that moved,
inching forward. The camera
became a part of him, tough pulsebeats
advancing like the blood.

He began to anticipate.
If a ball through a hoop
is a wish personified, it's his wish too.
He looks for symmetry, a promise that's made
in muscle and bone.

But sometimes he can see
that the organs will make the move, off center
like gritty magnets.

Maybe he'll focus on
someone who's lost this element,
the old-time baseball pro,
"yanked-out, disappointed, bent."

He has a feel for finishes.
He will pay out a hundred rolls of film
on deserted fields in the natural light
of summer afternoons,

or slow the speed at the end of the race
so that the runners appear to bloom
into a wide, deserved sleep.

For years he has been looking for
a vest with so many pockets
he can never run out of film.

THE CARDINAL

Again this morning I woke
as the cardinal banged
his head against the window,
slowly, purposefully, like
someone knocking. He does it
not to harm himself—we're sure
of this. He is only cracking
seeds for food. Or it may be
an accident. Witness
the bruises on my elbows,
my scratched hands. I myself
have no sense of where I begin
or end, like that dim lilac bush

that goes involuntarily
forward. You planted it
for someone else, without much sun
or hope. And if it didn't root,
well, one plant will always
take over from another. But it made
a thin connection here. I'd miss
that fragrance at the kitchen door.
Sometimes I find it upstairs too
in the deep closets where
her dresses hung. My own idea
about the cardinal is,
he's fighting for his life.
He sees an enemy, not just
that pale reflection in the glass.

RIVER BATHERS

This was no paradise.
The road bristled with ferns.
A tree threw its shape, headfirst
out of the shadows, so I saw
that there was water. We undressed
and went in. The human smell
fell away. Our limbs moved out
from the hub of the body,
so simply connected. Our skin
was a jumping-off place for light.
You could make a moral of this,
like the dazzle spinning off
Prometheus's hand: that water
completes us, that without it,
an animal is dust. From the far shore

rose factories and resplendent dumps.
I held up my head. I scissor-kicked,
remembering to take in breath enough
to get me through. Climbing out,
I passed bushes and vines
looking themselves as if they had just
stepped out of the water. And on
the closest lawns, strange flowers,
cannas and dark dahlias, circled
the grass and rusting iron furniture.

BADGERS

I had been told not to approach them
as they go at dusk over the fields
for worms and mice. Aware of me
the male might attack, holding me off
while the others escaped. But these three
or four, I have no fear of. They are
my own dark creatures, come with me
through the fields, shadows I have brought,
whatever feeds on the start of night.

from THE CULT OF THE
RIGHT HAND (1991)

THE ROCKING CHAIR

My father has just come in from work.
I am still small, my yellow hair
only starting to darken. He pats my head
as if for luck. I see he hates
this going out each day, away from us.
His face comes back a stranger's face,
sharpened by losses, the dark beard
grown in again, defending his cheek.
I throw my arms around his neck,
wanting to reclaim him. But he turns
to my mother who sits, with all her power,
at the kitchen table. The kitchen shines

in the darkening house. Soon I come
for its protection. I bring my father's gift,
a small maple rocker. My parents' voices
clash and fall like the clatter
of forks on the luminous plates. He won't
go back again, but she is making him.
What will become of us? she says.
I'm rocking fast. The chair draws back
and sends me up into their midst.
On and on they sit with their still feet.

The rocker moves like some mad horse.
It skims the smooth linoleum and hits
the cellar door. Open, sesame—I'm only
thinking it. The cellar opens magically.
The chair and I go hurtling down, an odd,
lopsided ride that strikes each step
into the dark. There is a cry. Overhead,
at last, the voices stop. My mother rushes

to lift me with trembling arms. Then, heavily,
my father comes. He grips the rocker,
wrenching it out from under me, and
wrestles it to pieces with his bare hands.

A HOLY DAY

At breakfast, my mother has me
turn on the gas of that cold stove
forgotten the night before. Because I am
a girl and small, this is a small sin. But
it spins me into the quickmoving world. We have

a long walk to the synagogue. I play a minute
in the arbor, in the fallen vines. Then,
as the others do, I reach and press a kiss
onto the metal case, shiny white like
the doorframe. It is a sweet word, a tickly
word to say, mezuzah. God lives here.

Inside, He hides behind the sliding doors.
The men sit close to Him. I am in back
among black dresses, breathing in
face powder and the smokey light. The men
begin to pray. Their backs are bent and

they are singing. Through the window I see
the twisting crabapple and its fruit that is
always small. God loves the men. He keeps
them near. God loves the old. Somehow I know
this chanting is the noise of dying. I am not

listening. I hear what I will always hear
at such a time, that stillness before the fire catches.

FIRE

The winter sky encircles us,
this little unit of conspirators,
this family. The backyard
ends so far from the house.
I find my four years
moving me further and further
from my mother's body.
I feel the chill that stiffens the ground
and the sleeping animals, hoping
that something of her reaches me,
at least the hot anger.

Some days the coal goes down
like black knuckles
knocking on the chute.
The fire leaps up, expecting it.

My mother stokes the furnace.
All day she straightens things,
when the wash is done, smoothing
even the obstinate cloth
with a warm iron. Each night
my father pulls his way unevenly,
lame foot after angry foot,
through the upper regions of the house.

The boys, out in the world,
practice to be men, while my mother,
in one brother's baseball jacket—
red, with "Spartans" on the back—
takes out the pliant and exhausted ash.

140

SPRING RITE

It is June. We stand in line
in the schoolyard under the sun,
singing. These are
our loudest voices of the year.
The teacher waves her arms
as if to hurry us.
I am looking down at our long,
continuous shadow. I wear
my dark pink cotton dress
with its diagonal ruffle
like the sash they give

to winners of a race. These days
seedlings in pots sit
on the windowsills of our classroom.
Slowly, they are moving,
green spokes of a machine
we cannot imagine. In our
silent reading book
a boy runs off with his dog, Rags,

and a hobo. Through high weeds
they go, over country roads.
I have never seen a country road.
We are in this line
like halted marchers. For how long
must we go on singing?

WILD ANIMALS

"Your hair is a wild animal,"
my mother says, as if it were
luxurious and valuable,
with a life of its own and
a secret nature. She only means
it should be combed. I brush it
till it sparks. Meanwhile,
she lays out two red coats.
Like the fire in us, they shame
my father when he walks with us.

We visit mother's relative alone.
From the el, we move
down avenues and stairs
to the basement where she lives.
The dark extinguishes us.
A widow half her life, she's dressed
in it, but for the white lace collar
at her throat. Each chair we sit in
wears its shroud of lace.
Half-blind in her dim home,
she still crochets. The white twine
leads her through her life.

Like elephants, she and my mother
move carefully around each other
in the little kitchen, making
supper. They talk in low,
incomprehensible voices. Sometimes
I understand: "This is my home.
They'll take me out of it feet first."
I'm moved aside like a twig

that has gotten in the way. I sleep
surrounded by them in the one big bed,
turning all night between enormous safety
and the fear of being crushed.

IN THE NEW WORLD

There is my uncle
pulling the blue Dodge to the side
of the road, first in a family
of ox drivers to drive a car.
He is a farmer. It is
the only living he knows
how to exact from this new earth.
He is taking his corn and eggs
to market over clear, paved road.

Next to him, my aunt
in a checkered housedress
peers out through the same
wide window. Their daughter
is in back, bright
sixteen-year-old they dote on,
an American. My uncle and aunt
are thin and grey as dust.
They have poured their color
into her: red health, the grain shade
of her hair, green eyes
open to all they can contain.

What has happened
is a flat tire, some puncture
of the usual. My uncle
will jack up the ton of metal
with the strength in his back
and clever new tools.
He is an upright man, student of God
all his days. Everything waits
for him to hold it up. Behind them

someone doesn't see my uncle
pull up along the curve. Suddenly
nothing will take them any farther.
The child is dead, the farm lost.

The woman must walk in pain
the rest of her life. For years
my uncle sits more still than anyone,
hands locked between his knees.

THE PRINT SKIRT

The zipper is the tricky part
although she knows it inside out.
Each morning she reunites
the cold metal, any time she is ready
to step out through a door. And opens
it for sleep and to change back
into herself after school. She lines up

the enormous red flowers. How bright
they are against the white piqué,
formless and somehow violent, like the blood
that spills from her body secretly
and changes it. The two back panels

join the front. She tries it on,
this skirt the shape of her. The print
wavers brokenly over her belly. Her two hands,
working only recently as a set, must judge
and smooth and unify. Then her leg presses

the thrilling pedal. The school assembly
may laugh at her when she walks in the line
of pastel shades and tiny buds and checks,
taking among them, even the boys, these
red flares. She stitches and rips. It will
never show, like teeth marks, where she tries
and tries again, like her mind learning
to worry through a thought or a desire.

1939

A woman takes a small girl's hand.
The leaves pull away and fall,
separate, stiff with color.
Out of the smokey, distant forests
the train brings its load of passengers,
the passengers, their burdens.
A horse nuzzles the fence of every field,
at peace within its boundaries.
There is the woman's beautiful fair hair,
a certainty that's braided into it.

Before them lies the station house,
its civil wood. At the crossing
the station master's wife aligns the bars
of any misdirected night.
A girl is walking by her mother's side.
She knows from fairy tales
the shape that evil takes—
stretched in shadow, giants, witches,
wolves—the weight of poisoned fruit,
the irrevocable claim of fire.

The hill twists and flattens.
The little girl looks at the funny hooks
of weeds, like fingers pointing down,
down. She hears the snap of branches
underfoot, the whistling stalks
that pull the air into
their tubular, dry bodies. Sometimes
in the wind the trees reach up
on tip-toe to the sky like tall, lost girls.

These are easy days. Heaven
comes to meet the earth
in such a bountiful accord. The sun
so neat it pulls the water taut
until the river shines. The two walk on
into the clouds, an ample white,
into a sky that has already forgotten them.

WEDDING TRIP

They wonder what it's like,
mountains arched before and behind them,
to live in the shadow of mountains.
The steep, perpendicular power, like some
magnetic force, holds them down,
turns them toward one another.

They sit in the square, at the last
outdoor cafe. Their backs are stiff,
not only from the cold. It's how
they are with one another. She rubs
her hands to warm them. If he
would cover them with his . . . "Where are
your gloves?" he asks.

She looks away. Two figures
in the clock tower venture out,
raising flat hammers in a simple,
parallel motion. He sees them too,
their iron capes, their patience,
their slow pursuit of one another.
For an instant the hammers pause,
undirected, as if there has been

a mechanical failure. Then they strike,
strike. At last the tinny air subsides
and the couple's view, which has shifted,
tilts back, evening the sound.
They will learn to live with cold,
with dissonance, to face the same way, to hold still.

ON MARKET STREET

In front of the department store,
in the full surprise of day,
a young girl is lying
on a white sheeted hospital bed.

At first there is only
the fact of her, an impediment
to be gotten around
like a statue or accident.

But I'm stopped by the arms that end
in dull blades, the stiffness
of the form under the sheet.

Dust and sun drift down to her.
I watch her eyes fill up with light.
Then, as if she's beckoned them,
heavy footed pigeons come.

How calm she is, like a painted saint,
like a miracle she is used to.
Someone throws money in the cardboard box
a woman holds. A small boy, too,

is hovering nearby. She
is theirs. They are glad for her.
Anyone would be, seeing their hopes,
though they twist, come to some use.

They bear her along
as if all the souls in the world
corresponded in number to the stars,
each in its own vehicle.

STREET MURAL

At the inside facing
of a bridge
where it rises away
from the pigeon-spattered pavement,
someone who is fifteen
has put a deer with velvet antlers.
It is looking back at him
over its shoulder.
It has the quiet, interested eyes
of his mother.

He has seen his name
sprayed across stone
like the name of a hero.
But something else
is at stake here, something
heavy with the weight

of anyone he has ever known
who has died. This is
an unlit, empty space
but he is not afraid.
He turns his back
to the unsafe street,
to dismembered, rusting cars.

Looking close, the viewer sees
there is no inside
to this deer. It is more empty
than a hunter's deer,
cleaned and trussed to a car roof.
Its hollow back

is only a reminder,
a saddle where the mind
can sit and think, "deer."
Farther on, a fawn
licks at the dots
on its soft, puzzled hide.

Small tender shoots poke up
green and yellow. Leaves
reach out from the sides of trees
almost anywhere, to keep
the deer alive. Some of the trees
appear to crash and fall
in the midst of these calm animals.
It does not frighten them.
All are painted
in the shiny cast-off skins
of showcard deer.
The scene is peppered
with red and blue songbirds.
In a real wood, their calls
would be a wild knocking
in the boy's heart he could wake to.

TEXAS DEPARTMENT OF CORRECTIONS

—From photos by Danny Lyon

1. CHRYSALIS

Almost transparent, their thin bodies
in the white prison pajamas,
faces dark under flapping hats.
The long, delicate wings at rest,
spread behind them. These are only
sacks of cotton, filling as they pick.

2. IMAGO

With day they wake
to better fields, richer growth,
shaking off
the soothing crust of insect sleep,
raw and new under another sun.

Nothing can hurry them,
the hours paced in unending rows,
staring down into the moist earth,
into their entrapment.
Only suddenly the shutter
is tripped, metal blades falling
like a small, harmless guillotine.

3. PRINT

At the top, a mounted guard
gives orders in slow, explicit
human speech. Light strikes,
producing the latent, still reversible

image. The moment scatters on the film,
a flickering incandescent white,
the black defense of earth
and the men's impenetrable bodies.

Some miles south windswept palms
are stopped like dark stars along the road.

IN GREECE

They saw the two chairs on the shore
then doubled back, following the line
of blazing white houses. Leaving
the car they sank a few inches into
the sand as if they belonged here,

and looked at them up close. Not
beach chairs but simple kitchen furniture,
bright with a peeling blue paint. They were
set at an angle, so that sitting in them
you couldn't look at each other. So far
apart you couldn't touch. Chairs where
fishermen mended nets or where their wives
could sit to watch the boats come in.

Maybe that day the man and woman
sat down in them and looked into the sea.
Maybe they only thought of that years
later. They didn't swim, not in such
complicated water. Far out the green
gave way to blue and then a stain
that shone like blood. Years later

they are sitting in a room. No room
is able to contain all they want from
one another. By this time strangers
have a claim on them and think of his body
or of hers as it pertains to them.

The chairs on the shore are waiting
there forever, like marble columns
holding up the past. That afternoon

they might have stayed but they could see
how poor a place it was, how no one else
was sitting by the water. And in the car
were heavy suitcases that belonged to
the people the man and woman would become.

DINNER AT THE HOLIDAY INN

Not much with me, a jacket and my book.
I'm shown the window table, the exhausted sky,
someone with perfect posture arranged at the piano.
She sways. The music follows her. It cannot help
itself. I watch her flowered smock, her hidden face
tilt back and forth. She isn't good

but blond and full of pep, needed here and good
enough. I go off somewhere in the book,
as real a place as being here. A smile plays on my face
for no one. The fat notes spring into the sky
like miracle plants. Clearly, this distance is no help—
the life I've left matched theme for theme on the piano.

Hammered shut, the dark wood cabinet of the piano
may be the coffin of mismanaged deeds, of good
ideas. Or else the woman is a midwife and I help
pull myself through by listening. In front of me, the book
is closed. I read the mystifying sky
and turn and turn, not sure of what to face.

To help, I make myself a map. The faces
at the tables, the window, the piano,
and tucked into the trees, these few rags of a sky.
Then someone brings me bread. I bite into the good
hard crust. Nearby, like me, a woman with a book
is raising it to ward off blows, to rest her eyes, to help

conceal herself. And farther on, an older couple, helpmates,
confidants. For many years they have been face
to face. Like reading from a book,
their rehearsed speech. I hear them over the piano.

They catalog how long each cancer takes, then have a good
laugh over that, a laugh directed at the sky.

The last hills fold into the dark that fills the sky.
I watch as with a sense of purpose now the help
light candles at the tables. So little good
the small flames do, except to halo every face
and each becomes a separate solemn icon. The hands on the piano
smooth over it an old song, a page out of a book.

The sky has been closed utterly, a finished book.
In the window, like a ghost in a jar, is my own face.
The busboys leave their busy lives and with the kitchen help,
come out for air, come out for good, come out to the piano.

SHELLS

In the heat, in the high grass
their knees touched as they sat
crosslegged facing each other,
a lightness and a brittleness
in their bodies. They touched
like shells. How odd

that I should watch them say goodbye.
What did it have to do with me?

There was my own stillness
and the wasps and the tiny flies
for a long time taking stitches
in the surrounding air and

a comfort I felt, as the wind
tore through, to find the trees
miraculously regaining their balance.

THE CULT OF THE RIGHT HAND

*—Ijo sculpture: Hand Cult Figure, rider of a monstrous beast (the soul).
His right hand is thought to be the source of his aggressiveness and skill.*

I. THE UPPER HAND

Each of us mounts his own soul,
a creature held up by impulse,
by avowal, by fantasies
of war: the spirits of ancestors,
mutilated veterans, horrific diseases.

We rejoice in the quick horn,
the muscles shining beneath the skin.
When his fangs lock, a door is shut
on our most damaging secrets.
Our enemies see in his dust
the sky rearing up in terrible punishment.

Because of his long legs
we make him carry us.
He'd rather graze the quiet fields
alone, moving slowly over grass.
In our right hands are reins,
in our left, the curved air of fear.

2. ENSURING THE WELFARE OF THE SPIRIT

After long drought
the herd stampedes,
excited by the rain.

A man loses his cattle,
goes mad, wanders naked
through the bush.
No one can go on like that,
a darkness
always weighing one side down——

forgetting spring,
the uproar of stars
in the northern sky.

The rest of us make peace.
The table is set, the grass mowed,
the teapot whistles to warn us.

Our voices climb higher,
stronger, in the steps
of song. The cup and the fan
are sacred in the temple of our grasp.

3. RITUAL METHOD

Not to let go.
To take flowered cloth
and wring from it a beauty.
To heat the quiet carcass
until it sputters and darkens.
To peel, to strip the toughness
from anything with the heart to grow.

To soothe the young
of any species,
picking discomfort from them
with light fingers.
To see that the night is full,
for peace of mind, to cover it from view.
To treat misfortune
with the charms of our strange beliefs.
To lock doors
and to shore up the earth
in backyards and gardens.
To keep in every closet,
every cupboard
something hidden of ourselves.

THE WILD PARAKEETS

In the evening she comes out
to the garden's ruthless growth.
Against her shears agave raise
invincible swords. She is overwhelmed

by the cannibal blossoms of bougainvillaea.
The water is pushing with all its weight
against the seawall. In a few hours
she will witness again what seems

the impossible effort of sunrise.
Nothing has noticed her, a widow, frail,
alone. Frogs in the grass are singing
to themselves. Not even the roaches scatter.

She works until her fingers ache, until,
clear of weeds, the jacaranda has been lifted up.
Then it may be a bird she hears or the iron
chirp of the empty swing. She tries to stand.

Out of the long-neglected lime tree,
wild parakeets swoop down at her
with their scalding voices. What is
this impulse, fierce and green? She's sure

the sun is at the heart of it. They
have escaped from someone's care into the heat
and light of Florida. Now free, they mate
and bear new young. Oh, shut them up,

banish them. Like the voices on the radio
that sing under her sleep all night.
But she'd take music, even music,
over this jangling dialogue.

from Toward Morning/Swimmers (1980)

SUMMER IN BODINES

Each day
I take the bike out,
riding deeper and deeper
into my own dark forest,

green,
wet with the eyes of animals.

I am following the dead,
their distant backs,
hoping they'll turn
and be themselves
when they see I know them.

The deer, in that new country
so still,
waiting for their names.

REMAINS

I remember when the days stood like this
with their backs to me.
There wasn't a single day
that happened from the front.

I know they held still
while the flesh was ripped from anything,
trees,

till the park lay before me with
its bones put end to end.

I sat reading in a chair
that faced the window,
the pages waiting to be turned.

I thought of what you took with you
in your haste,
what you left.

3

I am 3
flat in the long grass.
The sun hovers, wavers on its gladiolus stem
my belly pressed to the small yellow fires
of dandelions, buttercups.
Over me, dense
the bodies of insects heating up.

I hear my mother call my name.
It wriggles toward me
like a thin black snake.

POLIO

There was this disease
out gobbling up the children.

It grabbed us
around the chest,
beat at our limbs
with mangling wings

so bad
our parents
tried to snatch us back
as if we were in the path of buses

which meant
no swimming pools
no merry-go-round in Hunting Park,
or play with other children
who might be carriers

only the tin tub
on the front porch

echoing with water.

IN THE HOME

My mother sits in the small chair
that is now enough for her.

Her fingers find the edge
and tap, tap
as if there is something
she is trying to remember:

the way she liked to braid
her long thick hair

in the terrible rain
that shut us off
from all the other houses.

LEGACY

The apple trees above their solitary fruit,
the flowers that I know:
bittersweet, stiff with dying.

Why do I come?
She has a family here.
The grassy mound has settled into place
more on the level of the other deaths.

Meanwhile, at home
my mother has left silver in the drawer,
knives and forks crossed in their thin paper.
Enough for one small meal.

SHORE POINT

If I am small,
the night is very large
very full of everlastings,

on and on the sand completes itself:
each foot I lift
sinks in and asks a deeper question.

Hot, red as death,
the water shrugs and then
continues its mistakes.

You should be here
to look at me.

For the first time
I wake alone,
ocean, ocean
at the doors of my ears.

SWIMMERS

I see there is water
all around.

In the garden
the vegetables are swimming north

under the rivers of earth
red coal shuts its eyes

lovers surface
from the damp of kisses

the babies,
tied to us by breath,
knot their long wet ropes.

ACKNOWLEDGMENTS

Grateful acknowledgment is made to the following publications in which versions of some of the new poems appeared:

The American Poetry Review, "Noto"
Boulevard, "Hypothetical Architecture," "Late Afternoon"
Chautauqua Literary Journal, "Eidolon"
The Drunken Boat, "Sundowner"
88, "The First Time," "Break," "Mint"
Ellipsis, "Hyperstartle," "In a Couple"
Hotel Amerika, "Invitation," "Saltmen of Tibet"
Mid-West Quarterly, "Hunter's Moon"
Nimrod, "Twenty-three Weeks"
One Trick Pony, "Sheep," "Starwatch"
Parnassus, "Le Mépris"
Per Contra, "Betrothal at the Well"
Prairie Schooner, "Light and Heat," "Small Hours"
Red Clay, "Remember"
River Styx, "The Heap"
Shade, "The Pines: A Journal"
The Women's Review of Books, "The Lesson"

PUBLISHED BOOKS:

The Dog's Heart. Copyright © 2002 by Elaine Terranova. Reprinted with the permission of Orchises Press, Alexandria, VA.

Damages. Copyright © 1995 by Elaine Terranova. Reprinted with the permission of Copper Canyon Press, P.O. Box 271, Port Townsend, WA 98368-0271 www.coppercanyonpress.org

The Cult of the Right Hand. Copyright © 1990 by Elaine Terranova. Published by Doubleday, New York, NY.

Toward Morning/Swimmers, chapbook. Copyright © 1980 by Elaine Terranova. Published by Hollow Spring Press, Chester, MA

NOTES TO THE NEW POEMS:

p. 6 "Eidolon". The epigraph is from Elizabeth Morgan's translation of *Electra* in *Euripides, 2*, University of Pennsylvania Press, 1998.

p. 43 "Betrothal at the Well" was suggested by various passages in Robert Alter's translation of *Genesis*, W.W. Norton & Co. Inc.,1996.

p. 51 "Light and Heat". The epigraph is a modernized version of lines from Christopher Marlowe's *Doctor Faustus*:"Now body, turn to air,/ Or Lucifer will bear thee quick to hell!/ O soul be changed into small water-drops/ And fall into the ocean, ne're be found."

p. 44 "Sleeping Rats Dream of the Maze" is dedicated to Arlene Goldblatt.

p. 77 "Hyperstartle" is a term coined by Ronald Simons to denote extreme susceptibility to the startle reflex, in his book *Boo!: Culture, Experience, and the Startle Reflex*, Oxford University Press, Inc., 1996.

p. 83 "Saltmen of Tibet". The film documentary, *The Saltmen of Tibet,* was made by Ulrike Koch in 1997.

A thank you to Courtney Queeney who provided valuable editorial assistance on the present volume.